MW01152696

📱 813-712-3073

🌐 mobilizationfunding.com

Let's talk CASHFLOW

The

BIG BOOK

of

CA$H FLOW

UNLEASH YOUR COMPANY'S ULTIMATE
POTENTIAL FOR GROWTH AND PERFORMANCE

SCOTT PEPER

Print ISBN: 978-1-66787-095-3
eBook ISBN: 978-1-66787-096-0

To my wife, Jessica, and three amazing daughters, Kaylee, Chelsea, and Sydney – I love you so much and you mean more to me than anything else in the whole world. I love you!

CONTENTS

FOREWORD

I still remember the immense pride that coursed through me following the close of my first seven-figure construction contract. From my earliest days of construction sales to now leading my organization towards its largest project to date, this was a coveted moment to say the least. And while some may read these words and assume that what comes next is celebration and reward... those of you in construction know better . . . *what you close you've got to construct.*

The construction process is rarely straight lines and seamless assembly; it can be jagged, messy and downright defeating. The truth is, this monster project was all of those challenges and more. From the stress of how to scale up my workforce to the sheer anxiety of "Can I actually pull this off?" The pressure was immense. In fact, many of the tactics I use today in dealing with fear, lack of control and anxiety were forged throughout the course of the project . . . and all of this before you throw in the wrench of inadequate cash flow. This is where I got my first lesson in the "school of hard knocks for project funding." I fought through many sleepless nights and multiple bounced checks. I questioned everything, "Was this project just too big for me?", "Was I not making money?", "Is there going to be any profit? But as you may suspect, the problem wasn't sinking profits, it was negative cash flow. This is when I learned the cardinal rule of business finance: *Profits are Theory, Cash is Fact.*

While I wasn't sure of it, I made it through the project but not without learning my lesson. When the next big one came, I'd be ready. As is usual in the path of achievers like you and I, the next one did come, and it was even bigger! Determined to not relive the pain of the past, I sought out guidance from one of the brightest minds in construction finance I knew, my then newly found friend, Scott Peper. Scott, being the servant-hearted man he is, took the time to understand my business and the opportunities that lay ahead. Within a matter of days, he and The Mobilization Funding team evaluated my next big project (a multi-million-dollar deal) and helped me put together a cash flow plan that worked. The Mobilization Team saw the cash shortfalls and filled them with timely funding and a plan of execution that would ensure I stayed focused on doing great work . . . and that's exactly what I did. The principles you'll learn within this book are the catalyst that fueled my second record-breaking project to be on schedule, completely funded and producing an even bigger profit than projected!

So, while it is true, what you close you've got to construct, it's equal truth that what you construct you've got to fund. The tools needed for contractors to grow, scale, and fund their operations is exactly what Scott provides to you in the pages that follow. Aside from the finance-focused knowledge he's able to share, Scott is an incredible human who's always focused on adding value to those he has contact with. I'm honored to call him a friend and assure you he's lived up to his personal standards of unrelenting service and maximizing value throughout the pages of this book.

To those embarking on the journey of business building I commend you, I'm here with you, and know you'll be better prepared to seize the opportunities ahead once you've completed The Big Book of Cash Flow.

Andrew Ammons

President – ACR Commercial Roofing

INTRODUCTION

I WROTE THIS BOOK TO help business owners learn the importance of cash flow and how their understanding of this one piece will likely be the key to unlocking the secret door to the other side of their dreams for their business.

That cash flow will make or break them in business and if they focus on all the other things and avoid cash flow it will likely lead to failure and bring their dreams for their business to an end.

However, if they focus on cash flow and get it right most of the time (while still doing everything else) they will be much more likely to achieve the success they are looking for.

I didn't study cash flow or even finance in high school or college. I'm not a CPA or financial expert. For the longest time I wasn't even someone that focused on my own personal budget or cash flow at home.

Most of my experience comes from sales. Selling timeshares, gym memberships, and then ultimately medical devices. In selling you have conversations—you speak with people. If you do it correctly you should be listening the majority of the time. It's that listening that allows you to learn. Sure, the purpose might be to sell something but a byproduct of that is you learn a lot, too.

I listened to people from all walks of life. I learned what they did to make a living, how they achieved success, and what failures they overcame and how. When we started Mobilization Funding, I used those same listening skills when I spoke to contractors and other business owners. I learned from them what their problems were, where they struggled, why they struggled, what they did to try and fix it, how they adapted, where the problems occurred, and all of their "if only this could change or this existed" solutions.

It was in those conversations that the ultimate answer to the problem occurred to me—cash flow. "Cash flow" is an easy, generic term. But how cash flow impacts them is the real key. The solution was a tool that gave the owners the information they needed in a way they could use it.

A way they could see the information in their own way that was aligned to how they lived and operated—a way that was built FOR them. I learned they would make the decisions and changes needed when they were empowered with the information in advance. They had the ability to make proactive decisions that significantly improve their success—on projects and in business overall. It was amazing to see.

At Mobilization Funding we had the same problem. We were trying to make loans to these business owners to help them but we needed to understand how the cash would flow through the business and the project. We needed to understand that to make a good decision on whether we could help the business owner with a loan and if we could be paid back. We needed that cash flow to tell us how much money they need for the project, when do they need it, and when could they pay us back so that they would be in a better situation than when they started.

Those key items were in total alignment with the business owner's needs.

The cash flow tool was born for the MF loan program, but in that moment I realized it was really the perfect solution for all those contractors and other business owners I had listened to and learned from on all of those calls.

So we made the tool available to everyone. Then we made the tool even better. Then we created a digital version, so all business owners could access it. This tool has helped hundreds of business owners run their projects and business. There simply is no reason not to share this tool with hundreds of thousands of business owners, so that is exactly what we are doing now.

I wrote this book to create awareness about cash flow, to let contractors and business owners know someone out there actually understands, has created a solution, and has a passion and desire to share it with all of them.

A SEMI-FICTIONAL STORY

The following story is semi-fictional, an anecdote pulled together from the realities our clients have faced.

Joe Mitchell was a second-generation construction business owner. Lightning Electrical had grown under Joe's leadership from $1.5 million in revenue (11 employees) to what was now a $5 million a year business with 45 employees. But, Joe was still working for his same paycheck, despite all that growth. In fact, Joe had more stress, more sleepless nights, more problems to manage and people to worry about. He often wondered if any of this was even worth it and he wasn't exactly sure if he was earning the profit margin on each job that he thought he was . . . somehow there always seemed to be expenses popping up that he hadn't accounted for, eating away at the bottom line. His daughter was their office bookkeeper (and scheduler, and marketer). She wasn't a CPA. She kept records in QuickBooks. She didn't know why this kept happening either. Her solution was to increase his markup on every job, but Joe was afraid he wouldn't win any new bids and even lose business if he did that.

Worse than all this, Joe found he still had to scramble to cover the upfront costs of each new job. Everyone he knew in the industry seemed to have the same problem. It came with the territory—you won the contract, worked the job for 30 days, invoiced the GC, then waited another 30 days to get paid. You had to cover at least 60 days worth of labor, materials, and supplies just to keep the project going.

Joe was a licensed electrician. He had his OSHA certification. He knew how to successfully execute all the electrical needs for a commercial office space, a shopping mall, even a hospital. What he didn't know how to do was solve this problem of cash flow in his business.

But he knew *there must be a way.*

LET'S GET STARTED

We mainly work with commercial construction contractors and manufacturers, so most of the stories in this book—real or fictional—will be from those industries. But good cash flow management is important to businesses in all industries, and the tips and practices found in these pages will help any small business owner who finds themselves taking on more work but never feeling like they have any cash to show for it. If you have ever felt like this you are not alone and I wrote this book for you.

Before we talk about good cash flow management and share a few tips to improve cash flow at your business, let's back up a bit. What is cash flow, and why is it so important?

CHAPTER 1:

WHAT IS CASH FLOW

WHAT IS CASH FLOW?

IF YOU'RE NOT ENTIRELY SURE what we mean when we say "cash flow," don't worry—you're not alone. Cash flow is simply the money coming in and out of your business. **Positive cash flow** shows that your cash flow is increasing — more money is coming in than out. A positive cash flow means you can pay all of your company's overhead costs, debt payments, and other expenses, still have some money left over in the bank account and hopefully provide a buffer against any future issues or challenges.

If you have positive cash flow, you can reinvest in your business, take advantage of growth opportunities, and weather financial downturns with less stress. It is important to know the cash flow of your overall business as well as how each specific project or transaction contributes to your overall business' cash flow.

Negative cash flow, conversely, shows that your company has more outgoing money than incoming.

Cash flow can shift from positive to negative or vice versa from week to week or month to month. This is why proper cash flow management is so important.

Free cash flow is the money left over after all expenses are paid. Free cash is one of the most important aspects of cash flow management, as it determines your ability to grow, to recover from a bad project or a bad season. Free cash flow is the one to understand and manage the closest. It is the one that separates a stressful cash situation or not.

Free cash flow can also impact your team's performance. We'll get to that in Chapter Six.

Cash flow comes in three forms: operating, investing, and financing. We'll focus on operating cash flow, which is the money your business makes from selling goods or services. Basically, the money your company makes doing whatever it is your company does. Financial cash flow shows the money you use to fund your business, including debt, equity, and credit. Investing cash flow is money created from investment opportunities.

TYPES OF CASH FLOW

There are three major sources of cash—operations (company revenue), investments, and finance (loans, lines of credit, equity raise).

Operations cash flow is all cash generated by the purchase of your company's main service or product. Most of a typical contractor's cash flow will come from operations, *from the work you perform.* When you bill your customers or submit a pay app and then get paid, that's a primary source of cash. Consider if you have other sources as you prepare your cash flow statement.

Investment cash flow includes cash generated by investments in capital assets or other ventures. An example of this may be the interest charged on a loan to an employee or an investment made in another business, or it may be Bitcoin that you bought in the business.

Finance cash flow is the money you take in from debt or equity, less the payments you make on that debt or equity (known as "Debt Service").

WHY CASH FLOW MATTERS

Lack of cash is one of the most common reasons that businesses fail. Even companies that appear to be thriving and are highly profitable on paper can suffer from negative cash flow and ultimately run out of money, causing their business to suffer or even have to close.

By looking at your overall cash flow, you can see how profits, revenue, expenses, and working capital all relate to and impact each other.

CASH FLOW VS PROFITABILITY

Obviously not all of the money generated by your company's activities is profit, but it is all part of your cash flow. Knowing how much of the revenue generated is profit, or free cash, and how much must be reserved for expenses, is critical to cash flow management and the vitality of your business. This is especially critical when you are managing your supplies or payroll. Not managing cash correctly will often first show up in one or both of these places.

Cash flow is the movement of money in and out of a business; profit is the surplus after all expenses are deducted from revenue. So, which is more important?

Cash flow. Why? Because a business can survive without profit, but negative cash flow is a killer.

It is entirely possible to be profitable and have a negative cash flow. This is especially common if there is a long delay in payment. It is also possible to have a positive cash flow and not be profitable. For example, if a construction contractor company is taking on some additional debt or factoring their receivables they could likely create positive cash flow for a certain period of time. However, if the company's bids are too low to accommodate overhead and project expenses, or the company's debt payments or overall expenses are too high, the company will not be profitable despite the additional cash created by the loan or factoring.

Most business owners focus on profits and revenue, with good reason. But cash flow, and specifically your cash flow statement, is a more useful indicator to determine your company's financial health and how you feel about your company's finances on a daily basis.

For example, a company can experience an increase in profits while also suffering a dwindling bank account. Without cash flow management, this juxtaposition can leave business owners feeling helpless, uncomfortable, scared, and as if they are in a downward spiral.

CHAPTER 2:

CASH FLOW MANAGEMENT

CASH FLOW MANAGEMENT IS PARTICULARLY critical for small and mid-size businesses, as these companies often have less free cash flow to help them cover unexpected costs, delays, work shortages, or their growth. For these businesses, it may only take one project going south, or one poor financial decision, to bring an otherwise healthy business to its knees. That is the power of cash flow.

Here's an easy question: Do you know how much cash you have in your business each and every day, what the expenses of the business are that week and the next four weeks ahead, as well as how much cash you need to use in order to manage each of those week's needs? If you answered NO to all or any part of that then this is especially for you! (Checking your bank account at any given moment to determine how much cash you have is NOT sufficient to give a Yes to this question.) A report given to you weekly or daily as the business owner is key to your cash flow management success. The actual amount of cash in your bank account at a specific moment is different from the cash you actually have available to use. Cash in your account is only one piece of the equation. We will get into this later in more detail, but if you have ever heard someone use the phrase "managing the business out of their bank account," this is exactly what they mean and it is not good.

Managing your cash flow sources and the consequent uses of that cash can literally make or break your business. A U.S. Bank study showed that 82 percent of small businesses fail because of poor cash flow management. We cannot overemphasize the importance of being able to estimate, track, and forecast the money coming in and out of your business, especially if you are planning to grow.

Prolonged cash flow shortages can lead to insurmountable debt, while short but chronic shortages can lead to stricter payment terms with vendors and lenders, who no longer trust your ability to pay. It can also impact your company's credit score, which means banks will be less likely to lend to you when you need funds to grow … or survive.

The good news is that good cash flow management can positively impact your company's financial health and its projected growth, as well as your team's performance. It will also allow you to have a lot more fun in the business and avoid those stress-packed days. We'll get to that. Right now, let's break down a few easy steps you can take to improve your cash flow management.

UPGRADE YOUR ACCOUNTING

Are you still managing your own accounting? **Put this book down and go hire an accountant, possibly a bookkeeper too.** That sounds extreme, but effective accounting is seriously THAT important to your business. Don't rely on QuickBooks or your friend's mother-in-law, unless she is a Certified Public Accountant (CPA). You need a trusted professional who can help you navigate your cash flow statements, ensure you maximize your cash flow, and help you craft your business growth strategy. You need the CPA's brain to set it all up and then you can have your bookkeeper run the plays, with your CPA making sure everything runs smoothly at the end of each month. Find an accountant that works with other clients in businesses similar to yours so they have knowledge that can help you.

If you are saying to yourself, "I can't spend the money on an accountant" or "they are too expensive," then you either need a new accountant because the one you have is not helping you, or you are being penny wise and pound foolish. PERIOD. A good accountant often pays for themselves in a relatively short amount of time. After all, finances need to be current and accurate in order for you to stay on top of your accounts and plan for growth.

You also need to know your numbers. Whether you hire a CPA or not (please do), the first step toward better cash flow management is to know your numbers. You have to study something to understand it, and you have to understand something to affect it.

"Know your numbers" may sound cliché, but it is so critical to your success or failure. You have to know what costs you have in your business— the fixed costs (salaries, rent, debt service, insurance, vehicle payments, etc.) and the variable costs associated with your products or services.

If you use accounting software—or even better, if you work with a CPA like we mentioned above—you should be able to get an accurate breakdown of your cash flow sources and uses in a cash flow statement.

We all go into business for a completely different reason than "know your numbers" but that does not mean we get to ignore them. If you do your business will most likely fail despite your best intentions.

It is also important to know how you are tracking and recording revenue and expenses. **Accrual accounting** tracks revenue and expenses as they occur. In **cash-based accounting**, revenue and expenses are not tracked until cash is exchanged.

Cash-based accounting is considered easier by some, but in our opinion accrual accounting gives business owners a more accurate picture of the company's financial health. Either way, knowing how money is tracked will inform your analysis. We recommend you work with your accountant to find out what is the best way for you and your business in order to provide you the most accurate information you need to make good decisions.

CREATE A CASH FLOW STATEMENT

By looking at a cash flow statement, you can see if you are accurately marking up your products or services to cover the overhead expenses of running your business. Here's how you determine the accurate markup:

- Add the fixed cost of all recurring monthly expenses to get the total monthly cost. Multiply by 12 to get the Total Annual Expense of those fixed costs.

- Determine what the estimated Total Annual Revenues will be for the year.

- Divide the Total Annual Fixed Expenses by the Total Annual Revenues to get a percentage.

That percentage is how much of each dollar you sell will need to go toward paying your fixed overhead expenses. If you add that percentage—known as your "overhead allocation"—to every product, project, or bid you will break even and have no profit at the end of the year. What amount or percentage you add above that is what your actual net profit will be.

Fixed Cost of Recurring Monthly Expenses

Type of Expense	Monthly Cost
Rent or Mortgage	$5,000
Insurance	$6,000
Utilities	$1,500
Fixed Salaries	$17,000
Benefits - Health Care / Other	$1,700
Debt Service	$15,000
Total Monthly Fixed Cost	$46,200
# of months per year	12
Total Annual Fixed Cost	**$554,400**

Total Annual Revenue of Business $4,000,000

$$\text{Overhead \%} = \frac{\text{Fixed Exp (\$554,000)}}{\text{Annual Rev (\$4,000,000)}} = 13.86\%$$

The next step is to track your cash flow. This is especially true in businesses where costs can change. We specialize in working with construction and manufacturing companies, and their project costs can shift quickly and often. The same could be true for a restaurant, if the prices of ingredients suddenly skyrocket due to a shortage. Tracking your cash flow on a daily, weekly or monthly basis (depending on the nature of cash flow in your company) helps you stay ahead of any potential cash flow issues. We will discuss Cash Flow Tracking in Chapter 4.

Your first business cash flow doesn't have to be a complex document filled with formulas you don't understand. Start simple: What are your sources of cash?

15

HOW TO CREATE A CASH FLOW STATEMENT

If you have an accountant or use QuickBooks, you already have the ability to see a cash flow statement. (We have a free project cash flow template available on our website. Visit us at mobilizationfunding.com/cashflow to get yours!) In order to create a cash flow statement for your business, you need to know from where money comes into your business, and where it goes. These are the Sources and Uses, respectively, of your cash flow statement.

Sources

There are three major sources of cash—operations (company revenue), investments, and finance (loans, lines of credit, equity raise). Most of a typical contractor's cash flow will come from operations, from the work you perform. When you invoice your customers or submit a pay app and then get paid, that's a primary source of cash. Consider if you have other sources as you prepare your cash flow statement.

Uses

Now that you have your sources of cash, list out all the uses of cash in your company. Payroll, materials, insurance, fuel, all count as uses of cash. Don't forget the overhead expenses it takes to run your business—rent or mortgage, vehicle payments, utilities, supplies, marketing or advertising, etc. Consider the amount of each of these expenses, but also the timing and frequency you need to pay them. Overhead expenses are typically paid on a consistent basis (weekly, monthly, quarterly, or even yearly) while project expenses will occur variably (when ordered or per specific terms that can fluctuate the day they must be paid). For example, if your supplier gives you 30 day terms from when you placed an order then you may need to pay your supplier multiple times throughout the month.

Now that you have your Sources and Uses, enter them into the cash flow tracker template you have chosen. Ideally, your company cash flow tracker will be updated weekly, but for many businesses daily is necessary.

Once you have your monthly Sources and Uses laid out, sit down and analyze the data. What do you see?

Current Week	Week - 1	Week - 2	Week - 3
Week Ending (Date)	January 1st	January 8th	January 15th

	Week - 1	Week - 2	Week - 3
Beginning Cash Balance	$ _____	$ _____	$ _____
SOURCES of Cash			
Lines of Credit	$ _____	$ _____	$ _____
Other Loans	$ _____	$ _____	$ _____
Customer Payments (Accounts Receivable)	$ _____	$ _____	$ _____
Total Sources of Cash for the week	$ _____	$ _____	$ _____
USES of the Cash on Hand			
Payroll / Labor	$ _____	$ _____	$ _____
Contractor Payments	$ _____	$ _____	$ _____
Fixed Expenses	$ _____	$ _____	$ _____
Debt Service Payments	$ _____	$ _____	$ _____
Supplier / Vendor Payments	$ _____	$ _____	$ _____
Total USES OF CASH	$ _____	$ _____	$ _____
Ending Cash Balance	$ _____	$ _____	$ _____

WHY A CASH FLOW STATEMENT MATTERS

How you manage your company's cash flow can mitigate problems or compound them. Treat your company like a project, with a fixed budget and an approved list and schedule of expenses. (Actually, some of you may want to treat it better than a project budget.)

Many business owners evaluate their company's financial health based on their bank statements. Stop that. Your bank statement is not an accurate depiction of your company's financial health. It actually is just one small piece of your business' financial health. Think of it like this—in the same way that just because your heart is still beating doesn't mean you're healthy, neither does it mean that because you have a lot of cash in your bank account that your business is healthy.

A good understanding of your company's cash flow can identify gaps in cash flow, the problems those gaps will create and how you can create solutions proactively. Avoiding the immediate urgent problem in advance will allow you to have your life back and give you freedom to run your business and have your entire brain to do it. Can you have your customer pay you sooner? Should your next contract be negotiated differently to influence when you're paid or based on certain milestones that will allow you to better manage your cash flow needs? Those kinds of decisions impact the project and your organizational cash flow, and a cash flow sheet allows you to see those factors and make decisions from them.

Your customers, family, employees and their families are all relying on you to succeed. You can significantly increase your odds of success when you have the right information at the right time in order to make the right decisions. If you don't have the right information, or worse, you have the wrong or no information then it doesn't matter your experience or abilities—you are leaving too much to chance and the risk of failing or struggling is significantly higher.

Along with your cash flow statement you'll want to look at your income statement and your balance sheet. Your income statement is also known as a Profit & Loss (P&L) statement, and is focused on the revenues and expenses during a particular period. Your balance sheet reports assets, liabilities and stakeholder equity.

Together, these reports paint the picture of your company's financial structure and wellbeing.

WHY CASH FLOW MANAGEMENT STARTS AT THE PROJECT LEVEL

You have to spend money to make money, right? For many industries, like construction and manufacturing, that adage is particularly accurate. Each new contract means new expenses incurred *before* new revenue is earned.

It's tempting to see a signed contract as money in the bank, but it's not. Here's another adage for you: Don't count your chickens until they hatch. When it comes to cash flow, that would be *Don't count your cash until it's deposited.*

The cure for the "counting chickens" thinking is simple — a separate cash flow statement for every new project.

To show you how this works, let's say Big Rick's Roofing has a contract for $800,000. Owner Rick Davis knows he has about $250,000 in materials expenses and estimates labor will cost him another $350,000. Without a project cash flow statement, Rick has no way to determine when those costs will be incurred in relation to when he'll get paid.

But Rick is smart, and he builds an estimated project cash flow statement for every new job. He knows he will have to cover about $200,000 in expenses in the first month of the project. (That includes about $15,000 allocated to company overhead costs.) Expenses in Month Two will be about the same, for a total of $400,000. Rick estimates that he won't receive payment until Month Three, and that he'll probably only invoice for $150,000 in Month One.

This project has a serious cash flow issue. Rick has $125,000 in the bank and that isn't going to cut it. Besides, if he uses 100% of that money for this project only his company has no safety cushion until he can put the money back in the account.

In the end, Rick is able to use a bank line of credit and funding from a private lender (like us) to cover those costs. He builds the cost of the funding into a new project cash flow statement and sees the cost of borrowing the money he needs only reduces his margin on the project from 25% to 22%, an acceptable cost considering the opportunity of the contract and the overall amount of money he will make. Most importantly, he will be able to do the project comfortably while paying his labor each week, purchasing materials when they are needed, and renting the right equipment to the project in the most safe and efficient manner. Rick has now ensured that he will be able to sleep well at night!

The other benefit of project cash flow statements is they roll up to your organizational cash flow. When you know the timing of revenue in and expenses out on each individual project, you get a better idea of which projects are serving your company's growth and which are draining the cash tank. You may find out certain types of projects are much better than others and some customers are really not worth working with for your business. You also know which projects are contributing cash to the overall business, when they will be doing it, and if any cash in the business or from other projects will be needed to complete a certain job. You will also know when a specific project becomes cash flow positive on its own and you no longer need to contribute any cash to keep it rolling—at that point the project is in fact providing "free cash" to the overall business that can be used for general overhead, savings, to purchase capital equipment, or to invest in your team's performance and safety through continuous education or improvements to your work culture.

As we'll see in the next chapter, estimating cash flow on an organizational and more granular level is critical to building a solid financial foundation from which to grow.

Project Month   1

Total Contract Amount	$800,000
Total Project Expenses	$600,000
Total Margin	**$200,000**

- -

Project Costs

Direct Employee Labor Cost	$60,000
Subcontract Labor	$0
Material	$125,000
Equipment Rental	$0
Bond Premium *(if applicable)*	$0
Overhead Expenses	$15,000
Total Project Cost	**$200,000**

- -

Project Cashflows

SOURCES

Total Cash on Hand Currently	$0
Line of Credit - Open Availability	$0
Mobilization Funding Loan	$0
Receipt of Pay Apps from Project	$0
Total SOURCES OF CASH	**$0**

USES

Project Costs "PAID THAT MONTH"	$200,000
Payment Applied to MF Loan	$0
Total USES OF CASH	**$200,000**

Net Monthly Cashflow *(Surplus/Deficit)*   **-$200,000**

	2	3	4

$60,000	$105,000	$95,000
$0	$0	$0
$125,000	$0	$0
$0	$0	$0
$0	$0	$0
$15,000	$0	$0
$200,000	**$105,000**	**$95,000**

$0	$0	$0
$0	$0	$0
$0	$0	$0
$0	$150,000	$250,000
$0	**$150,000**	**$250,000**

$200,000	$105,000	$95,000
$0	$0	$0
$200,000	**$105,000**	**$95,000**

| **-$200,000** | **$45,000** | **$155,000** |

ANDREW AMMONS & AMMONS COMMERCIAL ROOFING

A Company Built on Excellence

Owner Andrew Ammons founded the company with high standards for performance, service, and results. With their commitment to excellence and over 10,000 clients served, it is no surprise that ACR Commercial Roofing is the industry leader in their area. Ammons has built a community in his company and beyond, founded on values of integrity, innovation, professionalism and accountability.

The Big Opportunity

Ammons and team won two government contracts worth $1.5 million. He estimated the job would take 13 weeks, but he suspected that if he had more working capital at the start of the project he could build in greater efficiency to the schedule and even save on some costs (specifically labor).

Time is money, Ammons knew. The faster he could get this job done—without sacrificing quality—the less labor expenses he would incur for the project. Get in, get out, get paid. But how could he do it?

Using our cash flow project tracker, he saw he was right. With a loan from us to finance payroll, he could put an additional crew on the job and increase the materials landed on the job in advance. He could accelerate the project schedule

The outcome? Ammons and his crew were able to finish the 13-week project in just eight weeks. That's five weeks of labor on the project saved which goes straight to the bottom line (more profit and increased margin.) In addition, that same crew can now get to a different job site and increase the productivity of that project.

But that's just the financial outcome. Ammons also says that, because he wasn't chasing down funds or stressing out over cash flow, he was able to focus his energy on building his business. During this project's schedule, Ammons rebuilt his estimating department and added some technology to help the team grow the volume of new construction bids to roughly $38 million dollars in that same time period. A significant increase for the team and now a very nice pipeline!

In His Own Words

"Not worrying about cash flow because you're covered with an army out there is a very good feeling for an owner or an operator. . . . Y'all's solution gave me the ability to focus where I needed to as a business owner." — Andrew Ammons, Ammons Companies

CHAPTER 3:

ESTIMATING CASH FLOW

USING HISTORICAL DATA AND BEST practices to estimate your company's cash flow, and the cash flow of an individual project, can make or break your company's growth and success. Whether you are a contractor, a fabricator, a restaurant, or a professional services firm, all businesses have some amount of new costs and need for cash.

Changing the menu for the season? You have new food costs. Running a fashion boutique? New items on the shelf equal new costs for you. Onboarding a new client to your marketing agency? Make sure you account for the cost of new customer swag. (We love good swag here at Mobilization Funding, and we invest in making ours awesome.) Every new construction contract comes with its fair share of costs before even a dollar of revenue is earned. It is those costs combined with the normal payment and cash flow cycle that makes construction particularly challenging.

Mapping out the estimated cash flow has many business advantages that can help you build success and grow your profit without growing your stress level.

- Spot upcoming cash flow shortages and solve for them in advance.

- Compare expenses versus income by month, quarter, year to identify trends that need to be addressed or changes that need to be made.

- Estimate the potential cash flow impact of a business change such as hiring new team members or starting multiple projects at one time.

- Demonstrate to potential lenders that you have the ability to repay their loan and positive cash flow.

ESTIMATING ORGANIZATIONAL CASH FLOW

Let's say you own a luxury baby apparel boutique and you have a goal to increase revenue by 25% as compared to the prior year. To reach that goal, you'll want to estimate the necessary additional expenses and cash needs in order to make that goal attainable and then track against those estimates all year. You will also need a budget, but that is for another chapter.

Step 1: Determine your cash flow starting point.

This is as simple as consulting your business cash flow report when you have one, but in the meantime, you will need to do a little work. Start with what is in your bank account(s) right now and add any additional sources of cash you have access to. Then add up all of the free cash flow from all other available Sources. (This would likely be Operational cash flow. Remember from earlier chapters this is from your customers paying you.) Next, you will need to choose a specific date to start from—oftentimes it makes sense to start with the end of the previous year because you should have a clean set of financials and/or a tax return that states specifically where you are at that period in time (December 31st). Then you can use that specific year as your "baseline" to project forward from.

CASH FLOW STARTING POINT

Bank Account(s) ending balance

Account 1 $ _____

Account 2 $ _____

Line of Credit Available Balance $ _____

- -

Total Available Cash to Start $ _____

Step 2: Estimate incoming cash flow for the next period.

Based on historical cash flow tracking of Year A (the "baseline"), you can make a rough estimate of what the expected revenue will be for Year B.

Be sure to account for any anomalies, positive or negative, in the historical data. For example, if your company was closed for several months due to the shutdowns related to the coronavirus pandemic, that will have a negative effect on your cash flow data that should not be repeated.

Similarly, if you worked on a particularly large project—something way outside your normal scope—it is best to mark it as an outlier in terms of estimating cash flow. On the other hand, if you do have one-time events that you know are typical each year then you should account for those too.

For example, you are going to purchase a truck this year or you know one of your customers is going to order in bulk at the beginning of the year versus consistently every month like in previous years. These are the kinds of things to think about when planning in this stage of the process.

Estimating INCOME for Year B	Jan	Feb	/ /	Nov	Dec	Total
Current AR Detail						
Customer 1	$					$
Customer 2	$					$
Customer 3	$					$
Customer 4	$					$
Total Current AR by Month	$					$
Future Estimated AR						
Customer 1	$					$
Customer 2	$					$
Customer 3	$					$
Customer 4	$					$
Total Future AR by Month	$					$

Step 3: Estimate outgoing expenses for the next period.

Just like you did with your revenue, you'll want to review and tally up all of the expenses from the baseline period in order to get a rough idea of what you will spend in Year B. In a perfect world you will estimate revenue and expenses at least on a monthly basis to start and plan for the year—then refine this down to weekly looking ahead 13 weeks at a time. Then as each week goes on you add a week to the 13 so you always have a 13-week "look ahead" of the cash needs of the business. The week you finished becomes what actually happened and you adjust the weeks coming up and add one more week to the end. This allows you to always have a line of sight to the next 13 weeks of your business.

Estimating EXPENSES for Year B	Jan	Feb	/ /	Nov	Dec	Total

COST OF GOODS SOLD (COGS)

	Jan	Feb	Nov	Dec	Total
Product or Service 1	$				$
Product or Service 2	$				$
Product or Service 3	$				$
Product or Service 4	$				$
Total COGS by Month	$				$

LABOR

	Jan	Feb	Nov	Dec	Total
Direct Employee	$				$
Contract Labor	$				$
Total Labor by Month	$				$

OVERHEAD AND ADMIN

	Jan	Feb	Nov	Dec	Total
Rent / Mortgage	$				$
Utilities	$				$
Insurance	$				$
Total Overhead by Month	$				$

DEBT SERVICE

	Jan	Feb	Nov	Dec	Total
Loans	$				$
Equipment	$				$
Other	$				$
Total Debt Service	$				$

Step 4: Subtract the estimated expenses from the estimated revenue.

This one is pretty self-explanatory. Just like when you're creating your cash flow statement, you need to subtract your expenses from revenue in order to arrive at your estimated free cash flow. This will give you the projected cash balance to end the period of time you are planning for.

Estimating INCOME for Year B	Jan	Feb	Mar	Apr	May	Jun	Jul	Aug	Sep	Oct	Nov	Dec	Total
Current AR Detail													
Customer 1	$50,000	$25,000	$20,000	$0	$0	$0	$0	$0	$0	$0	$0		$95,000
Customer 2	$10,000	$10,000	$5,000	$0	$0	$0	$0	$0	$0	$0	$0	$0	$25,000
Total Current AR by Month	$60,000	$35,000	$25,000	$0	$0	$0	$0	$0	$0	$0	$0	$0	$120,000
Future Estimated AR													
Customer 1	$45,000	$45,000	$45,000	$45,000	$50,000	$50,000	$50,000	$50,000	$50,000	$50,000	$50,000	$50,000	$580,000
Customer 2	$25,000	$25,000	$25,000	$25,000	$25,000	$25,000	$25,000	$25,000	$25,000	$25,000	$25,000	$25,000	$300,000
Total Future AR by Month	$70,000	$70,000	$70,000	$70,000	$75,000	$75,000	$75,000	$75,000	$75,000	$75,000	$75,000	$75,000	$880,000
TOTAL AR	$130,000	$105,000	$95,000	$70,000	$75,000	$75,000	$75,000	$75,000	$75,000	$75,000	$75,000	$75,000	$1,000,000

Estimating EXPENSES for Year B	Jan	Feb	Mar	Apr	May	Jun	Jul	Aug	Sep	Oct	Nov	Dec	Total
COST OF GOODS SOLD (COGS)													
Product or Service 1	$43,500	$34,750	$31,250	$22,500	$24,250	$24,250	$24,250	$24,250	$24,250	$24,250	$24,250	$24,250	$326,000
Product or Service 2	$5,000	$5,000	$5,000	$5,000	$5,000	$5,000	$5,000	$5,000	$5,000	$5,000	$5,000	$5,000	$60,000
Total COGS by Month	$48,500	$39,750	$36,250	$27,500	$29,250	$29,250	$29,250	$29,250	$29,250	$29,250	$29,250	$29,250	$386,000
LABOR													
Direct Employee	$20,000	$20,000	$20,000	$20,000	$20,000	$20,000	$20,000	$20,000	$20,000	$20,000	$20,000	$20,000	$240,000
Contract Labor	$7,500	$7,500	$7,500	$7,500	$7,500	$7,500	$7,500	$7,500	$7,500	$7,500	$7,500	$7,500	$90,000
Total Labor by Month	$27,500	$27,500	$27,500	$27,500	$27,500	$27,500	$27,500	$27,500	$27,500	$27,500	$27,500	$27,500	$330,000
OVERHEAD AND ADMIN													
Rent / Mortgage	$2,000	$2,000	$2,000	$2,000	$2,000	$2,000	$2,000	$2,000	$2,000	$2,000	$2,000	$2,000	$24,000
Utilities	$1,000	$1,000	$1,000	$1,000	$1,000	$1,000	$1,000	$1,000	$1,000	$1,000	$1,000	$1,000	$12,000
Insurance	$1,000	$1,000	$1,000	$1,000	$1,000	$1,000	$1,000	$1,000	$1,000	$1,000	$1,000	$1,000	$12,000
Total Overhead by Month	$4,000	$4,000	$4,000	$4,000	$4,000	$4,000	$4,000	$4,000	$4,000	$4,000	$4,000	$4,000	$48,000
DEBT SERVICE													
Loans - Term	$2,500	$2,500	$2,500	$2,500	$2,500	$2,500	$2,500	$2,500	$2,500	$2,500	$2,500	$2,500	$30,000
Vehicle Payment	$500	$500	$500	$500	$500	$500	$500	$500	$500	$500	$500	$500	$6,000
Total Debt Service	$3,000	$3,000	$3,000	$3,000	$3,000	$3,000	$3,000	$3,000	$3,000	$3,000	$3,000	$3,000	$36,000
TOTAL EXPENSES	$83,000	$74,250	$70,750	$62,000	$63,750	$63,750	$63,750	$63,750	$63,750	$63,750	$63,750	$63,750	$800,000
NET INCOME (CASH)	$47,000	$30,750	$24,250	$8,000	$11,250	$11,250	$11,250	$11,250	$11,250	$11,250	$11,250	$11,250	$200,000

Step 5: Estimate your starting and closing cash flow for the period.

You can now see your estimated opening and closing cash flow statements for Year B. Let's break it down in an example.

You ended Year A with an available cash flow balance of $250,000. Your Year B estimated revenue is 1,000,000. The estimated expenses for Year B are $800,000. Your estimated available cash flow is $200,000, and your closing cash balance is $450,000 ($250,000 from Year A and the additional $200,000 from Year B).

Now you have your starting point or opening balance and your estimate.

Estimating cash flow is not an exact science, especially when you are planning out an entire year. When you are looking at it yearly, that is more of a budget in our minds than a cash flow tool, but you need your budget to know where you are going to start from. Remember that these are your best guesses based on the data at hand. Stay flexible and regularly check in on your cash flow estimates as part of your cash flow management practices.

CASH ON HAND CALCULATION

End of Year "A" Cash On Hand	**$250,000**
Year "B" Estimated Revenue	$1,000,000
Total Expenses Year "B"	$800,000
- - - - - - - - - - - - - - - -	- - - -
Expected Year "B" Cash Flow Created	**$200,000**
Cumulative Cash Year A & B	$450,000

Consistently checking in on cash flow is something you want to do on a weekly basis, at a minimum, if not even daily. Again – we recommend you use a 13-week cash flow tool to manage the cash of the business.

ESTIMATING CASH FLOW BY PROJECT

When you have the cash flow of every project estimated and scheduled, you have a solid foundation on which to build your business's profitability. Whether you use one provided by QuickBooks or your accountant or download our free template, once you have a working cash flow sheet template you can understand proactively the cash needs of a project—how much cash a project will need and when in the project—and even use the information to impact your processes when estimating and bidding a project.

First, in the Sources section of the cash flow tool, enter in when you expect to submit your invoices for the project. Put the dollar value of each invoice in the section or cell for the week you anticipate submitting the invoice. If you are a contractor, look for a cash flow tracker that will auto calculate your pay apps net of retainage. Otherwise, deduct your retainage percentage from every expected pay app. Your cash flow tool should have a function for when you will actually be paid by your customer. If you submit an invoice and are paid the next day then you can count the cash the same week you invoice, however that is typically not the case and your customer likely pays you a number of days after you invoice them. Your cash flow tool needs to be able to have the functionality to show when that money is coming into the business. Or you can just use the one that we created and have on our website for you (https://mobilizationfunding.com/cashflow/).

Next, enter in your weekly projected project expenses in the Uses section. It is important to input your expenses in the week you expect to incur them. Just like we discussed for the Sources section, your cash flow tool needs to have the functionality for you to be able to adjust what your vendor terms are (i.e. when you need to pay your vendor for what you ordered). Hopefully, you have terms and don't have to pay everything at the time you order, but this is important when projecting the cash needs of a project.

Once you have entered in your Sources and Uses, the cash flow tracker should auto-calculate the project's gross margin in dollars and as a percentage. This is great to see in one section summarized. It can also be very misleading because it assumes if all the work got done today and you were paid tomorrow that is how much cash you would make. The summary does not tell you how much cash you need to **invest** (Yes, I specifically used the word "Invest" on purpose) into the project in order to actually make that margin. That is what the rest of the cash flow tool will tell you and it is the main and best function of it.

The summary allows you to review your expected margin to make sure you are actually going to make what you expected when you estimated the project. It will also now show you how much cash you will need to invest in the project to get it started, when or IF the project will cash flow itself, and where the cash flow shortages are. In the event there is a shortage on the project you can then determine how to fill that shortage with other sources of cash you have in the business.

From there, you can update the Sources and Uses section with weekly incoming and outgoing cash flow. This gives you a granular view of when cash flow shortages happen. Once you can see how big or small your cash flow deficit is expected to be and *when it occurs,* you can strategize solutions to cover the gap.

PROJECT CASH FLOW PROJECTIONS

Project Week	Week 1	Week 2	Week 3
Week Ending (Friday)			
Invoice or Pay Application DATE to be Submitted			
Less Retainage			
Projected Net Pay App to be Submitted	$		
Project Costs			
Direct Employee Labor Cost	$		
Subcontract Labor	$		
Material	$		
Equipment Rental	$		
Bond Premium (if applicable)	$		
Misc. - Material	$		
Total Project Cost	$		
Project Cashflows			
SOURCES			
Cash Disbursements	$		
Receipt of Pay Apps	$		
Total SOURCES of Cash	$		
USES			
Project Costs "Paid That Week"	$		
Other SSV Payments Required	$		
Alternative Loan Payment	$		
Payment Applied to MF Loan	$		
Total USES of Cash	$		
Net Weekly Cashflow *(Surplus/Deficit)*	$		

Week 4	Week 5	Week 6	Week 7	Week 8	Week 9	Total
						$
						$
						$
						$
						$
						$
						$
						$
						$
						$
						$
						$
						$
						$
						$
						$

CHAPTER 4:

TRACKING CASH FLOW

BY PROJECT

The purpose of tracking cash flow is to know how much cash you have to spend at any given time in your business or project. It provides you with the data and information to make most of the important decisions on any project—when to start, how many crews can be put on the project, when to order material, type of equipment you can use, and so on. We created our Project Cash Flow Tracker (see Appendix) because we knew it was important for contractors to see how project expenses marry up to the job schedule and exactly how much cash is needed each week. The same is true for your organization. The cash you have in your bank account isn't necessarily the cash you have free to spend. You need to know when cash is needed, what it is needed for, how much is needed, and where it is going to come from.

Tracking cash flow across your entire organization can also help you break the habit of relying on one project's cash flow to start a new one — "borrowing from Peter to pay Paul." Instead, you can estimate costs for a new project, analyze your current cash flow statement, and make informed decisions about, (1) how you'll fund that next big job, (2) what happens if you are given notice to start that big job a month sooner, or a month later than planned,

(3) what if your next three jobs all start at the same time, (4) do you need to leave all the cash in the business or can you take an owner's distribution, (5) can you take on another project and if so what terms do you need to include in order to execute it properly.

Tracking cash flow by project makes tracking the cash flow in your overall business easier, and when you understand and are managing the organizational cash flow you will be able to manage your future project cash flow estimates much better. Your bidding and estimating process will be helped greatly.

To track cash flow across a project, first determine how cash moves in and out of your project. Are the costs and payments monthly, weekly, or a combination? In construction, the payments from a project are typically received monthly, but the expenses can occur anytime, and most often aren't due at the same time payments are received. And that's if the contractor gets paid on time.

You can use the same cash flow template you created in Chapter 2 to track project cash flow. In fact, it's a great exercise to see in real-time how the project shapes up against your estimates, and what exactly impacted the project's cash flow.

Over the last 9 years running and operating Mobilization Funding the project cash flow tool has become a real game changer for clients. If right now you feel like you're trapped on a hamster wheel of debt and stress, if you feel like you just can't get ahead no matter how much work you win and execute, if you are constantly thinking, "If only my customers would pay on time I'd be all right," then project cash flow management and more specifically, the project cash flow tool, may be the tip that breaks the cycle.

If the thought of a project being delayed a week, or a month, keeps you up at night; if you chase payments all week just to cover payroll on Friday; if you feel like each bigger project is a risk more than an opportunity because you don't know if the company can cover the costs—project cash flow management is going to change the way you feel about your business.

When you have the cash flow information you need—down to the granular, weekly level on each project—you can make decisions with clarity and confidence. You'll know exactly how much you need to start a new job and how much you'll need each week in order to finish it with a profit. You will KNOW the consequences of delays, the impact of increased production. You'll know how a change order will affect not just your schedule, but your cash flow, and so you'll know what to charge for the new work to cover it.

Best of all, you'll know payroll is covered, the business is not just growing but thriving, and hopefully you'll finally take home the owner's distribution you deserve for your own hard work.

ORGANIZATIONAL

Creating a cash flow statement and tracking cash flow across projects and throughout the organization can be a real eye-opener. It can reveal cash flow gaps in advance, as well as highlight some areas where you could conserve cash.

Many business owners are focused on "the work" of their company. They're in the weeds, at the job site, or on the plant floor, ensuring that the work gets done. That sounds great, in theory, but the reality is that someone needs to be in the driver's seat of your company—and that someone is You. It is admirable to be on the job sites and in the weeds with your team, and that needs to be done from time to time, but never at the expense or in lieu of the company's driver's seat.

We've already talked about the importance of working with an accountant. Just the exercise of walking through your cash flow statement with your CPA is beneficial. Having a solid controller in your business is very helpful and in many cases even better on a day-to-day basis than your accountant. Organizational cash flow management helps answer questions such as: What do I need to make my business run? Where may I be overspending? Can I reduce overhead or renegotiate supplier terms in order to increase profitability?

Like all things in life, you can't improve your cash flow until you are keeping track of it.

CHAPTER 5:

FORECASTING CASH FLOW

FINALLY, WHEN YOU HAVE A history of cash flow tracking and analyses under your belt, you can start to forecast or predict your cash flow, which is the key to making an effective cash flow plan for growth. You now have the ability to run your business and make good decisions in the moment but also proactively. Decisions like when to buy new equipment, bulk order supplies when there is a good deal, take an owner's distribution, hire a new employee, give bonuses, etc.

HOW TO FORECAST ORGANIZATIONAL CASH FLOW

The first step is to decide how far out you want to forecast. You want to plan out as far in advance as you can, but if you operate in an industry like construction, remember that change happens often and fast. Also, the newer your company is the less historical data you will have to build out your forecast so you will need to make assumptions as to what you can do with what you have at the moment. We recommend doing an annual forecast or budget that is broken down monthly. Then as each month closes out the numbers are compared to the forecast and become "actual" versus "forecasted." That month becomes an "actual" month in the forecast and the future months are still forecasted. This allows you to track the month's actual performance to the forecast and know where you stand to the annual forecasted plan as you complete each month. This budget is an important step because it will become the basis for how you track your performance throughout the year but also it will become the basis and structure for how you track cash in and out of the business.

To start this forecast you can use all of the high-level line items from your income statement to build a forecast (budget) for the year. For example, you do not need to guess what all your projects will be and a breakdown of each one of them for a year in advance. You should, however, be able to take your best assumption of the revenue you will invoice on a monthly basis (sources of income), estimate your project costs (also known as Cost of Goods Sold or "COGS") using a percentage of the revenue, your labor as a percentage of revenue, and so on. What I mean by that is if materials are supposed to be about 40% of your job and labor is 40% of the job then use those percentages when you build the budget template. The overhead expenses of your business should be able to be forecasted more accurately because they are fixed costs (salaries, insurance, rent, utilities, etc..) and then any debt service you have (mortgage on property, payments to loans, etc…).

Let's start with the top line revenue first. How much will you invoice on a monthly basis? This should not be what you *hope* to do but more of what you reasonably think you will do based on your current contracted work and an estimate of the future work you will win. This is critical because your entire budget will be built from this starting point.

A quick side note: This is where a lot of folks make a mistake in this process and in business overall. They know what their costs are and then they come up with a number they must invoice every month (or think they do) in order to maintain their business and bring cash in to pay the expenses on the business. Yes, it is important to bring in enough cash to maintain the business but not necessarily when you are building a budget. If you are honest in what the top line revenue of the business will be based on the work you have or can likely win then you can build the expenses of the business from that revenue. At that point you can see if the current expenses of the business are too high for the expected revenue. That does not necessarily mean you have to cut expenses, although it very well may be the right decision. What it *does* mean and will show you is that you don't have enough revenue to support the current operating expenses of the business. Now you can make a choice to cut expenses or raise cash to fill in the gaps. This is a small example of the power of a budget and cash flow template. Now let's get back to building the top line revenue target for the budget.

List all your sources of income (Sources). There should be one type of income for each row on the spreadsheet (example might be project revenue, service call revenue, etc…). Next, create a column for each month of the year. Don't forget your non-sales income like tax refunds and investments—this usually shows up on your income statement under "Other Income" if you use accounting software like QuickBooks.

Now it's time to list all your outgoing expenses (Uses of cash). Just like with your income or Sources, you want to create individual rows for each type of expense.

For both Sources and Uses, you want to enter in the data in the month when you incur the cost or actually receive the money. Not when you get the bill, not when you sign the contract, not when you send the invoice. Only when the money lands in your bank account or leaves it.

You know what to do from here, right? Deduct your net Uses from your net Sources for each month to see if you have a positive or negative cash balance for that time period. Too many negative periods mean your business has a cash problem, but the question is what is the problem and why?

This could mean your expenses are too high for the revenue of the business currently, the work you are doing is being bid at too low of a margin, the margin you thought you had on projects and were bidding is not accurate, or it might just be that the business needs to get through a certain period of time (a couple months or a quarter) before the cash catches up with the business. Considering you have the data in front of you now you can also start working on solutions NOW—before you are in the middle of a problem.

If you're in the black for the forecasted period, congratulations! Now is the time to scrutinize the model and find out if there are any adjustments you need to make and if all things are coming out as you planned them.

Annual Budget Template	Month of Operations	Jan	Feb	Mar	Apr
SOURCES	**Contract / Revenue Terms**				
Operations (Project Revenue)	Progress Billing (as laid out in contract)	$70,000	$30,000	$50,000	$20,000
Operations (Service Revenue)	Monthly Billing	$20,000		$20,000	
Investments					
Finance					
	Total Sources	$90,000	$30,000	$70,000	$20,000
	Annual Income	**$644,000**			

– –

USES	**Payment Terms** (Net 30, COD, Paid When Paid, Weekly, etc.)				
Direct Costs					
Payroll	Weekly	$8,000	$8,000	$8,000	$8,000
Subcontractor	Paid when paid	$11,000	$8,000	$15,500	$2,500
Materials	Net 30	$70,000	$25,000	$8,000	$35,000
Insurance	Monthly	$1,000	$1,000	$1,000	$1,000
Fuel	Weekly/Daily	$1,500	$1,500	$1,500	$1,500
Overhead					
Rent/Mortgage	Monthly	$1,500	$1,500	$1,500	$1,500
Vehicle Payments	Monthly	$1,200	$1,200	$1,200	$1,200
Utilities	Monthly	$500	$500	$500	$500
Supplies	As Needed	$150	$150	$150	$150
Marketing/Advertising	Monthly	$400	$400	$400	$400
	Total Expenses	$95,250	$47,250	$37,750	$51,750
	Cash Flow Surplus (Deficit)	-$5,250	-$17,250	$32,250	-$31,750
	Annual Profit / Annual Income	**$138,500**			
	Net Profit %	**22%**			

May	Jun	Jul	Aug	Sep	Oct	Nov	Dec
$65,000	$40,000	$22,000	$77,000	$38,000	$42,000	$60,000	$10,000
$20,000		$20,000		$20,000		$20,000	
$85,000	$40,000	$42,000	$77,000	$58,000	$42,000	$80,000	$10,000

- -

$8,000	$8,000	$8,000	$8,000	$8,000	$8,000	$8,000	$8,000
$10,000	$3,000	$4,000	$7,500	$3,000	$6,000	$5,000	$4,000
$40,000	$6,000	$25,000	$15,000	$10,000	$7,000	$12,000	$2,000
$1,000	$1,000	$1,000	$1,000	$1,000	$1,000	$1,000	$1,000
$1,500	$1,500	$1,500	$1,500	$1,500	$1,500	$1,500	$1,500
$1,500	$1,500	$1,500	$1,500	$1,500	$1,500	$1,500	$1,500
$1,200	$1,200	$1,200	$1,200	$1,200	$1,200	$1,200	$1,200
$500	$500	$500	$500	$500	$500	$500	$500
$150	$150	$150	$150	$150	$150	$150	$150
$400	$400	$400	$400	$400	$400	$400	$400
$64,250	$23,250	$43,250	$36,750	$27,250	$27,250	$31,250	$20,250
$20,750	$16,750	-$1,250	$40,250	$30,750	$14,750	$48,750	-$10,250

The next step is to now build the cash flow model off of your budget. The cash flow model is different than the budget. Although they go hand in hand and have a similar look and feel as it relates to the Sources and Uses items, there are some key differences to the cash flow model:

1. It will be tracked weekly versus monthly, meaning the columns at the top will be weeks instead of just months. This is because cash coming into the business at the beginning of the month is not the same as cash coming into the business at the end of the month. That budget you just built looks great but that assumes all the money comes in on day one of the month and expenses go out on the last day. We all know that is not the case in business, so we need to look at cash on a weekly basis.

2. The Uses section needs to be in greater detail and list out each vendor. For example, if the budget has a line item called "Materials" then the cash flow model will have that same category called Materials and all the materials vendors listed underneath that section.

3. The same goes for the Sources section. Income is the main category (like it is listed on the budget) but each source of income (your individual customers) should be listed underneath that category.

4. The time period you are tracking does not need to be annual. The most common time period is 13 weeks. So that means that the columns at the top of the sheet will be weeks and not months and they will only predict 13 weeks into the future. The reason for this is you are using your cash flow model to track the flow of cash in and out of your business and more importantly **how you need to use the cash you have when it comes in.**

Okay, now you have the templates for your budget and your cash flow model, and you are ready to manage the business with the data in front of you. Regardless of how the data looks—good or bad—it is the data and accurate based on what you know about the business and the facts you have in front of you. You are now empowered to see the good and the bad and have the ability to impact the changes needed to help you run the business.

If you are in the black on your budget and your cash flow model is positive with cash, Congratulations! Now is the time to put a purpose to your earnings and start planning your growth strategy.

PLAN FOR GROWTH

Growth is great, but growth without cash flow to support it can actually be a killing blow to your business. Sacrificing profitability for growth is like digging a grave and thinking you are building a castle. You're not, and eventually you're going to get buried.

You need a cash flow plan that covers your present needs and your growth goals.

Uncontrolled growth is one of the top reasons contractor businesses fail. In the race to win more bids and execute on those contracts, well-intentioned business owners push their company over a cash flow cliff. Growth is critical to long-term success, but if you are bidding too low on projects just to win them and grow the top line, you are doing more harm than help to your company.

Please read that last sentence again!

Taking on projects in a new geographic region or that involve work your team is unfamiliar with is exciting. It is also a potential profitability nightmare. Without the cash to cover the costs of setting up your operation somewhere new (including potentially increased supplier costs and transportation or even lodging for labor), you could find yourself working at a loss. Those costs need to be factored into the project and/or you need to make sure you have the cash on hand or a source of cash to cover those costs as they occur. Growing is awesome and you should want to grow. I'm here to point out that when you grow, how you grow, what jobs and work that you do to grow, and *how you manage that growth is the key to actually growing.* There is a top and a bottom line on your income statement for a reason—focusing only on the top does not mean that the bottom line grows too—actually oftentimes it is quite the opposite.

Profitability and growth have to go hand-in-hand. That means building out cash flow plans for every project to ensure each job will eventually sustain itself and close out with a profit for you.

Cash flow is also in that list of construction contracting business killers. Cash flow in construction is complex—with high costs around new work, protracted payment schedules, and a constant cross-stream of money in and money out as pay apps are approved and vendors are paid. A lot of contractors compound the issue by running all of their cash through one checking account and not implementing a defined, 13-week cash budget. You have to know where your sources of cash are coming from, and what expenses or uses of cash are expected each week. Otherwise, it is nearly impossible to know how much free cash flow (funds not earmarked for another expense) you have on hand at any one time. And if you don't know how much you have, it is even harder to know how much you will need in the future.

Some of you may be reading this right now and saying to yourself, "I never have any extra cash." Or, "When I do have a little extra cash it is for something else." I know the feeling and so do most folks in business at one point or another in their journey.

The most important thing to know in those moments is WHY! Why is there no extra cash after all the work is done? You will be able to answer that question when you track your cash flow and you will be able to make corrective actions on a project or in the business to change that. The types of changes you will make are (1) how you set up your bids, (2) what jobs you take, (3) what jobs you don't take, (4) which customers you will work for and which you won't, (5) how you set jobs up, (6) who you hire, (7) the material suppliers you choose, and the list goes on.

This may seem crazy and sound like a business that isn't yours, but I am here to tell you it can be your business too. Think about how easy for you it would be to say, "NO" to a project or a certain customer if you knew that every time you worked on a project like that or for that specific customer you lost money or made ½ the amount you do on every other project. And if you hadn't done any of those types of projects last year or any with that certain customer you would have had 25% less top line revenue but made 25% **MORE** net income. Yes, made more money doing less work.

This happens all the time and we see it in our business every week when we work with our customers. It seems silly, but it is NOT. How can you expect to answer those kinds of questions for yourself from just a gut feeling or a hunch and be confident it was the right decision? Now imagine you have that gut feeling or hunch and it's supported by real data and information. Now you are in the driver's seat of your business and making the best decisions for your family, your employees, and their families too!

CHAPTER 6:

USING CASH FLOW MANAGEMENT TO SUCCEED

CASH FLOW MANAGEMENT ALLOWS YOU to make strategic decisions regarding your company.

- How are you going to spend the cash in the bank account right now?
- How much do you need for payroll this week? Next week? Four weeks from now?
- Can you order the material you need right now?
- How should payment for the unexpected repairs on equipment be made?
- When is the next round of cash coming into the business and how much is it?
- Where do you want to be next month or year?

The data will not only show you if you need to make changes in the company, but also which types of jobs are most profitable for your company and should be on your target list for growth.

With good project cash flow management, you'll also know you can take on those new projects, how much cash you'll need to do them right, and how you will finance those expenses. And that may be the greatest benefit of cash flow management — the confidence that your company is secure, successful, and growing.

STOP CASH FLOW STRESS

In Andrew Ammon's testimonial video, he mentions, " . . . the value of sleeping at night." He's right. Good cash flow management can give you a sense of assurance and confidence that your project, and your company, is on the right track to succeed and grow.

That peace of mind doesn't show up on an Excel spreadsheet. There is no entry field for it in QuickBooks. But if you are the owner of your company, you know how important your own mental health and wellbeing is to your business. You know that when you are not in crisis management mode you can make a real impact on your business, and your people, that will help everyone succeed collectively.

Effective cash flow management means you can let go of the fear of upside down project earnings. You can also stop chasing down customers, begging them to pay you now or even early, or "borrowing" from one project to pay for another. Instead, you can do what you are supposed to do—lead your team to victory. Set the strategy for success and then empower and incentivize your team to execute that plan.

When you're not worrying about cash flow, you can be the leader you were meant to be.

SET AMBITIOUS AND ACHIEVABLE GOALS FOR GROWTH

You need a cash flow plan for your business' regular operations, for every project, and as part of your growth strategy. It's the only way you will be able to see where you are now, where you want to go, and how to get there.

Uncontrolled growth and poor cash flow are a result of inadequate planning. To achieve the growth goals you set out, you need a strategy that includes a financial plan that covers the cost of the growth.

Leverage all of your options when building your financial plan for growth. Is there overhead that can be reduced? Can you negotiate better terms with suppliers? Every dollar you can save is a dollar you don't have to cover in your growth plan, making it that much easier to reach your goal.

One key mistake many contractors make is the desire to self-fund their growth. This is an important lesson successful business owners learn early — funding your growth by borrowing capital isn't "bad debt," it's a smart investment. But it's only smart when you know how to use it, what you will use it for, how much it will cost you and you have the framework and tools in your business to manage it properly. **That is the difference between being successful with debt or allowing the debt to destroy your business.**

The tools you need and the information on how to use them are all available for free to you as a business owner so there is no longer an excuse not to have them. People and companies are providing the education and access to information business owners need via the internet—YouTube, podcasts, social media, and even this book are a great start to help you! Check your resources of information very carefully. Be sure to go to sources who are doing or have done and accomplished what you are trying to accomplish. There are a lot of fakes and frauds out there that have never done anything but are ready to tell you what to do. Look for resources from your accountant, lawyer, local small business development center (SBDC), trade partners, suppliers, etc.

Finally, analyze which types of jobs are best for your profitability. Don't necessarily rely on only asking other companies that are in your space what jobs are the "best." Take the time to analyze the data in your company with the projects you have done and with the customers you have worked with. Industries and companies have many similarities, but they don't have all the same nuances, people, and cost structure that you may have in your business. Where there is opportunity for others there may not be for you, and conversely where others struggle you may have the best opportunity. The data in your project cash flow will answer those questions for you. Then you can target the GCs who offer those types of projects when you are bidding work and targeting new customers to work with. Find your sweet spot and dig at it until you strike gold.

Growth can't be avoided—in business you are either growing or dying. Grow with a cash flow plan that supports you, your team, and your clients so you are able to grow with confidence. You can also live with a lot less stress too — growing your business does not have to be so stressful you can't sleep or hurts you mentally. Remember, it is not something you have to do alone. Find the talent inside your organization and if it is not already there then you can find it outside and either contract for the help to learn or hire the talent you need.

OPERATE FROM ABUNDANCE

This is a mindset shift, a SKILL you can learn, not a tactical strategy. When you work from a place of scarcity, you are always assuming that you don't have enough. That something will go wrong. That you "lack" something. The result is that you feel stress associated with what you are lacking, the mistake you might make or the thing that will go wrong. You are not the only one that feels it either; your team feels your stress and they in turn become stressed as well or worse nervous and scared. The GC or customer probably feels your stress, too. They don't know why you are stressed, they just assume that it can't be good and it could hurt them so they start to protect themselves naturally by insulating you and your team. You can't truly do your best work, because you are operating at a disadvantage.

This may sound hard to do . . . and it is. Business is hard too and what you are trying to accomplish is also hard.

Everything is hard. But, hard doesn't mean impossible. And it doesn't mean unworthy. Some of the hardest things you'll do in your life are the most worthwhile. Like running your own business.

Now that we have established that I want to share one more thing with you—you are 100% going to make mistakes, 100% lack something you need, and 100% it will cause some stress of some kind. Now that we have established that IS going to happen you don't need to let it burden you. The key to handling all of those things is focusing on what you ARE going to do and what you CAN control. That is why these cash flows and management of cash in your business is so critical. The methods to do it are tried and true and when you are armed with the information it provides you are able to make good decisions much easier.

Here's how that shift looks: Operate from a place of abundance. Know the baseline profit margin you MUST earn in order to complete a project the RIGHT way. Then, bid on more of those jobs. Keep bidding those jobs till you land them and grow from there. Doing work for free or for little to no profit just is not worth it.

Don't be afraid to have a higher price than competitors.

Read that line again. Compete on your VALUE, not your PRICE. Don't sell price as value. Sell VALUE as value. VALUE is your performance and the experience you leave someone with after they work with you.

You may not win every project, and that is okay. You will win the jobs that matter, that move your company forward and help you cement your reputation as a skilled and knowledgeable partner that people can trust.

You will be focused on performance, not price, and the results will show in your work. Your customers also care first about performance and less about price. Yes, they care about the price they pay, but they certainly care about the job getting done right first—a low price with a bad job or poor result doesn't help them or the customer they are serving. And over time as you execute those jobs and finish them those same positive results will show up in your bank account and your stress level!

In closing, do you want to make your life simpler and your business more successful? Of course you do. **The way to do that is solve problems for your customer and make it easy for them to please their customer.** You do that one thing and your customers will give you more business at the price you need.

ROBYN DONALDSON AND RENEW CONSTRUCTION CLEANING SERVICES

A Force for Good

Robyn Donaldson is a FORCE in the Tampa Bay construction scene. She's a business owner, a leader driven by purpose. She focuses on doing the right thing, providing the best experience to her customers, and giving back to her community.

The Small Business Catch 22

But, Robyn had a problem. She had a great opportunity in front of her, but her company was already bleeding money. There was no way she could make the payroll on this new project. But, she needed the project to grow.

It's a problem most small businesses have; they have the opportunity but they don't have the cash flow bandwidth.

Robyn connected with Mobilization Funding, and immediately her situation felt different.

The Result

Yes, we funded her project, but Robyn herself says that was only a small part of the relationship's value. We helped her organize and track her organizational cash flow and build a plan that got her company on an upward trajectory.

And that growth had an impact beyond her business's bottom line. Robyn was able to hire additional employees, creating a ripple effect of positivity throughout her local community.

In Her Own Words

"Something that you gave me is an ability to dream, or to scale. Because the thought of money, or being able to finance a project was my biggest fear. I never went after big contracts, because I just couldn't do it. But now that I have you guys, the sky's the limit." — Robyn Donaldson, Renew Construction Cleaning Services

CHAPTER 7:

CASH FLOW TIPS

CASH FLOW MANAGEMENT TIPS

Every business shares a common need: Cash. It pays the bills, it keeps the lights on, it puts food on the table, and it makes sure you are able to pay your employees. Cash isn't just king — it's LIFE. Which means cash flow management is like eating your spinach and exercising every day. It's the healthy regimen your company needs to keep the lifeblood flowing. Here are our best tips for better cash flow management.

Get your internal team aligned

We recommend working with a CPA, but it is also important, depending on the size of your business, to have a good accounting team or person. Communication is key for cash flow management to work. If you are not getting the reports you need, work with your team member or CPA to get them.

Your accounting team and your project teams need to start talking, too. Weekly team meetings is probably one of the most important things that you can do. Include your project management team with your accounting team. You might be thinking, *Yeah, right. There's no way my project team and my accountants can be in the same room together.* If that's true, then it's even

61

more important to get them in a room together. A business works as well as the people within it, and your accounting team can't operate effectively without input from your field team.

A transparent and clear line of communication between accounting and project management is key for both parties to see how their decisions impact each other. If an initial estimate had 100 square feet of tile, and now you need 400 square feet of that tile, your accounting team needs to know if the project manager is getting a change order for the extra 300, or if the company is eating that cost. Because if it was an estimate problem or your company is absorbing the cost for some reason, your cash flow just went down by 300 square feet of tile, and it is your accounting team's job to budget for that.

Negotiate terms

If you need something, you NEED to ASK for it. Remember that the customer/supplier relationship works both ways. You need their products; they need you to stay in business and keep paying them for the products they provide. If you need credit or extended payment terms, you need to ask for it. Get them invested in your success by sharing how the new terms will help you grow and order even more.

Get paid on time

The best way to avoid a cash flow shortage is to get paid when you expected to. In construction, the wait to get paid is often 60 days or more. One easy way to keep cash flowing in is to create a process around submitting invoices so that they are correct and on-time. In a world with many things you can't control, control the things you are able to. One of these things is your paperwork. Make sure it is accurate, in order, and submitted on time. There is no excuse for not controlling what you can!

It can also be helpful to set up reminder emails to clients if you have extended terms of payment. If you are required to sign "paid when paid" language then you need to make sure you are prepared in the event it takes a longer time to be paid and do not take on too many projects with those terms if it will hurt your overall business.

Build an emergency fund

Free cash flow is cash that you do not have to spend on overhead and that you could re-invest into the business. This is the ultimate indicator of financial health. Most accounting professionals recommend you keep three to six months of working capital in reserve. If this seems daunting, start small. Sit down with your cash flow analysis and determine what percentage of your cash can be saved. Then continue to save that percentage even as you grow.

Build efficiencies in schedule

Cash flow is one of the most important factors of your construction company's success. Good organizational cash flow management provides financial security for today and the stability to grow in the future. Cash flow also impacts performance. Specifically, the cash available for a project has a direct impact on your team's ability to do its best work.

The majority of delays in construction are due to cash flow. Can't fund payroll? That's a cash flow problem. Not enough funds to rent the Big Crane? Cash flow problem. Hurricane rips through town and destroys the site? Okay, that one is not a cash flow problem, but you still need some cash to keep paying your team while the site is down and the project is delayed.

Forecasting your project's weekly cash flow will help you spot the "danger zones," the weeks when cash is tight, you're nervous about making payroll, and/or you spend the week chasing down people that owe you money. Spotting those danger zones in advance allows you to proactively manage them before they are a problem and gives you the chance to come up with solutions in a much more controlled and less urgent manner. There are lots of proactive solutions: explore your financing options, negotiate different terms with your suppliers, or discuss the schedule with your General Contractor.

That's right, talk to your General Contractor. About money. Seriously. Listen—your GC wants you to do your best work so they have a successful project. You share a common goal. Bring an issue to them proactively, with an idea of how to solve it, and they are more likely to thank you than judge you. Bring them the same problem when it is in the middle of the job and it's a different story.

And if they give you grief, send them our way. We speak to GCs and our customers together all the time. I promise you the people you want to be working with care about performance and you first and foremost!

Tightening overhead

This may be as simple as cutting technology subscriptions or adjusting the thermostat, but often reducing overhead means letting people go.

Take a deep breath, this one is hard.

You need to balance permanent staff and contract workers. Even harder, you need to take a look inside the office. Is your payroll bloated with specialized staff members who do only that one job or don't do their job well enough? Would you be more profitable if you combined roles or outsourced a few of these duties? If you have people on your payroll that you have to pay whether there is work or not, you need to make sure they are (1) necessary, and (2) helping the business grow. Get lean and efficient to increase profit margins.

Nobody likes to let good people go. It is not a reflection of them or you—it is just part of running a profitable business. There is no business if the business can't support itself. Be the boss they'll never forget by helping them find their next opportunity. Help them write their resume. Give them a good recommendation. Leverage your network to help them find their next position.

Important note: It may be that you don't have to let people go. It may be that you are paying people way too much for the role they have in your company. Make sure you are paying your team what they are worth, but also that it is in line with the position and role they have. If it is high then perhaps they can do another role or their current role can be expanded.

FOR THE CONTRACTORS: MARGIN VS MARKUP

How does your business calculate the right bid for a job? Do you sort out the job cost and then increase it by a third? Do you use the "10 and 10" method, adding a 10 percent overhead and 10 percent profit? Are you able to differentiate between margin and markup? When was the last time you double checked those figures? Does adding 10% to the costs of a job even cover your overhead?

Financial expert George Hedley estimates that at least three-quarters of installation contractors don't know how to estimate the markup they'll need to cover job costs plus overhead and still turn their projected profit margins. Larger companies may find that their markup needs to be higher to cover increased overhead costs or to ensure that current or future investors are seeing healthy profit margins.

Understanding the difference between margin and markup is critical for business owners. Let's do a quick review now.

Markup Formula

For contractors bidding on jobs, calculating markup looks like this:

Bid Amount - Job Costs = Markup (in dollars)

Divide your markup by your bid amount to get your markup percentage.

We also see a lot of contractors calculate markup by starting with their total project or job costs, specifically labor and materials. Let's assume they use the "10 and 10" method as outlined previously. The contractor will take their total job costs and add 10% for overhead and another 10% for profit. At that point most contractors would feel they are safe with "20% in the job."

There are a few flaws in this method. First, you need to know what your total overhead costs are and if in fact 10% will cover them. For the time being let's just assume they do. Next, we want to make sure we have that 10% profit we expect to make in the job. Let's look at an example:

- Project costs are $800,000

- 10% for overhead = $80,000

- 10% for profit also = $80,000

- The total bid is $960,000 ($800K in job costs plus $80K in overhead and another $80K in profit) and includes $160,000 in markup

- Here is the issue: $160,000 / $960,000 = 16.67% in the job, not the 20% you thought you had.

10 & 10 Mark-up Method

Total Project Costs	$800,000
Add 10% for Overhead	$80,000
Add 10% for Profit	$80,000
Total Bid	**$960,000**

- -

Total Mark-Up (%)	20%
Total Mark-Up ($)	$160,000
	($800,000 x 20%)
Actual Margin %	16.67%
	($160,000 / $960,000)

Why does that matter?

Let's say that the same project has the standard 10% retainage being held back from every pay application. That will equal $96,000 from your contract amount. $960,000 - $800,000 in job costs - $96,000 in retainage being held equals $64,000.

$64,000 is *the only free cash flow you will see from this project* till you are paid your retainage. If you need $80,000 to cover your overhead then $64,000 is not going to cover you.

If you then borrow money to help manage the short fall or get the project started the cost to borrow that money will have to come out of the $64,000 as well leaving even less for overhead.

So, if you ever felt like you have "20% in the job" and can't seem to locate where it is, now you know where it is!

SCOTT PEPER

10 & 10 Mark-up Method

Total Project Costs	$800,000
Add 10% for Overhead	$80,000
Add 10% for Profit	$80,000
Total Bid Amount	**$960,000**

- -

Total Mark-Up (%)	20%
Total Mark-Up ($)	$160,000
	($800,000 x 20%)
Actual Margin %	16.67%
	($160,000 / $960,000)

Same Bid but calculating Margin instead

Total Project Costs	$800,000
Add 10% for Overhead	$80,000
Add 10% for Profit	$80,000
Total Bid Amount	**$960,000**

- -

Total Mark-Up (%)	20%
Total Mark-Up ($)	$160,000
	($800,000 x 20%)
Actual Margin %	16.67%
	($160,000 / $960,000)
Retainage at 10%	$96,000
	($960,000 x 10%)

Available Cash on Project

Total Bid Amount	**$960,000**
Retainage at 10%	$96,000
Total Project Costs	$800,000

- -

Cash Available on Project	**$64,000**
	(6.67% of Bid Amt)

68

This is why we recommend contractors stay away from using the markup method and instead think in terms of margin and free cash flow – we will tackle how to use margin in a few paragraphs from now.

For other businesses, calculate markup by taking the sales price of your good or service, minus the unit cost, and divide that number by the unit cost. Your unit cost is the total amount needed to produce and sell "one unit" of your good or service.

Margin Formula

First thing to note is there are two references to Margin: (1) Gross and (2) Net, similar to the references to Gross Profit and Net Profit.

Gross Margin is gross profit (top line revenue minus all job costs) divided by revenue. For a contractor bidding on a job, that would look like this:

Bid Amount - Job Costs = Gross Profit / Bid Amount = Gross Margin%

If calculating Net Margin, it would look like this:

Bid Amount – Job Costs – Overhead = Net Profit / Bid Amount = Net Margin %

For contractors this is a better method when bidding projects in order to make sure you are calculating the actual profit and overhead you are setting out to achieve. Once you win a job the process is fixed and very specific. The processes for getting paid, determining the schedule of values, retainage being held, payment to vendors, and so on. That process all starts with your contract value and works backwards from there. Each month you complete a part of the job, invoice a portion of the contract, and retainage is then held based off of the contract amount you invoice. This is why it is so critical to make sure to estimate and bid projects knowing what your margin and profit is as it relates to the contract amount and NOT the job costs, so that you actually have the overhead and profit you intended to have in the project.

Here is how that would look using the same example as we did in the markup section of this chapter:

- Total job costs are $800,000.

- At the end of the day, you want to have 10% of the contract amount for overhead and another 10% for profit.

- To solve for what the contract amount needs to be you need to do the following:

  ◊ Start with 100% and subtract the overhead % and profit % you want to achieve (in this case 10% for each).

  ◊ 100% minus 10% minus 10% = 80%.

  ◊ Now take you total job costs ($800,000) and divide them by 80%.

  ◊ $800,000 / 80% = $1,000,0000.

  ◊ $1,000,000 is the contract amount you need to bid in order to have 10% for profit and 10% for overhead.

  ◊ $1,000,000 contract amount

    » 10% overhead = $100,000

    » 10% Profit = $100,000

    » 80% job costs = $800,000

Now when you have 10% retainage held of the contract amount you still have enough in the contract to cover your overhead.

Margin Method / Formula

Total Project Costs	$800,000
Overhead % Desired	10%
Profit % Desired	10%
Project Costs as % of Bid	80%
Total Bid	**$1,000,000**
	($800,000 / 80%)

- -

Total Margin (%)	20%
Total Margin ($)	$200,000
	($1,000,000 - $800,000)
Actual Margin %	**20%**
	($200,000 / $1,000,000)

- -

Bid Amount	$1,000,000
10% Profit	$100,000
10% Overhead	$100,000
Project Costs	**$800,000**

If retainage is based off the Bid Amount in the field then you **MUST base everything else off that Bid Amount as well.*

You might be saying, "I'll never win jobs if I bid that high." That very well may be true and if so you will need to make some adjustments to what you bid, how many bids you get out in a given week or month, or the type of jobs you bid. At the end of the day the purpose of this exercise is to KNOW what your actual numbers are. To NOT be in a situation where you think you have "10 and 10" in the job and you don't. Or worse, you end up not making money or losing money. I would bet you win more jobs than you think and if you do the other things we have discussed in this book like evaluating your overhead, changing your mindset, and focusing on the performance and not the price you will win even more.

Common terms defined:

Job costs include everything you'll need to complete the work. This includes direct employee labor, sub-contract labor, materials, leased equipment costs, debt service / cost of capital (if borrowing money specifically for the project), bond premiums, permits, gas, lodging, per diems, and other materials and supplies. Basically any cost or expense that is directly spent on that project.

Overhead is all the bills and expenses not included in the above job costs that you will need to pay in order to operate your business. While this sometimes varies, it includes things like rent for your office, office-based support staff, some types of insurance, tools, equipment, bookkeeping, accounting, legal costs, owner's salaries, outstanding debt payments and whatever else it might take to keep the lights on if you don't have active jobs. Basically all expenses that are not directly attributed to a specific project or job account.

Net Profit is the remaining amount after job costs and overhead are subtracted from the price. Net profit builds cash in the business called Retained Earnings and is a direct sign of the health of a business. With net profit you can make capital investments in the company (new office, new equipment or machinery) and take distributions from the business or pay out bonuses. A healthy construction business should be able count a net profit of at least 8%, according to what some experts say.

Markup is the sales price, minus the job costs. Margin is the sales price minus the job costs and minus overhead allocation.

Here's an example:

Let's say you're bidding on a job that will cost your company $200,000 to complete with materials, labor, and equipment, and you plan to bid $250,000. Your total sales forecast for the year is $1 million and your annual expected overhead costs at that level is $80,000. That's an 8 percent cost of overhead. In other words, you need to tack on more than 8 percent to the cost of the job just to break even.

At the end of the day, having too thin of a margin can leave your company vulnerable if something goes wrong on the job, like a weather delay or another trade's issue. A good bid is never about just tacking on some standard percentage to your job costs. It's about being precise about your business's financial needs.

SCHEDULE OF VALUES

This section is for our contractor readers. The Schedule of Values a construction contractor builds is just as important to the project's success as the bid. It also can help you get paid faster, retain more margin, improve your cash flow, and even improve your team's performance.

That's a lot of VALUE hidden in your Schedule of Values. To cash in on all of that power, you need to build your Schedule of Values with the same strategic consideration that you apply to your initial bid.

Building a valuable Schedule of Values

Get granular. If you are installing the windows in a five-story apartment building, think about the time it takes to haul windows up to the second, third, fourth, and fifth floor. How many times does a crew member have to come back down? If you have the same labor rate and time for each floor then you are going to lose money on one or more of those floors. After all, it takes more time for your team to get up and down, wait on the elevator, deliver material, or even just run back to the truck from the higher floors. Think about it like this, if you were in a dispute and needed to justify why your costs are higher or you need a change order to be approved you would certainly want to have your Schedule of Values reflect the higher cost of what you are doing from the start. It cannot take the same amount of time to bring material to the 4th floor of a building as it does the first floor, so account for that when pricing out each line item on the Schedule of Values you build and submit. Get specific. Make sure your ability to invoice isn't contingent on another contractor's performance. If your plumbing company is laying underground or foundational piping and the original Schedule of Values defines "complete" as "Capped & Sealed," your invoice might very well be reliant on the concrete pour schedule. Align your Schedule of Values as close to your job schedule as possible, so you get paid for the actual work you did during that application period (i.e. month) and within guidelines that are within YOUR control.

Get confident. Just like your bid, you need to be able to show your work when you submit a Schedule of Values and it needs to be easily verified as complete so you can get PAID. Leave as little room for subjective interpretation on the line items as possible. Be thinking, "To do a great job I need my money to be paid to me in order to maintain the quality work you expect of my company."

Be careful where you put your margin

When you build out your Schedule of Values are you putting most of your project's margin in material line items? It seems like an easy win, especially if you can negotiate good supplier terms.

Unless something goes wrong, like the cost of material goes up, or materials get cut from the job, or the General Contractor decides to buy the materials themselves.

Don't leave your profit margin up to chance! If you put your profit margin in certain line items and remove it from others, then you need to make SURE the overall margin you intend to make is still there when you invoice.

It's construction; a lot can go wrong, and at least one thing definitely will. You need to make sure that you are able to get some profit billed into every invoice; it's the life blood of your business.

Also, if you are putting your margin in certain line items, you better let your Project Manager know. They need to be aware of how that next materials order, or any Change Orders they receive, will affect the margin on the job. Project management and accounting and finance need to be communicating regularly and working together.

How else do you spread your margin? You could add a percentage to every line item, or you could boldly list it in your bid. This is a power move. It says to the GC, "I know what my company is worth and what it takes to do the work we do." You might be surprised too. Many general contractor's perception is that subcontractors are making A LOT more than they actually are. You could put your total profit on the Schedule of Values and just OWN it like a BOSS. At the end of the day if what matters most to win the job is the final price then who cares.

If that route feels a little too bold, take a look at your project's Cash Flow Projection (you now know how to build one) and spread your margin across line items so that your project cash flows itself faster and stays profitable throughout.

How would you do the job if money were no object? It's not just a daydream; it's the first question you should ask when creating your bid and your Schedule of Values. This is where the efficiencies are and possible overall savings in cost. If money was no issue would you run the job differently (schedule, work force, equipment, etc…) and would it allow you to make more money by saving time and being more efficient? Hard to think that way when you feel like you never have enough money but the reason you are reading this book, especially this far into it, is because you want to think differently, and you want someone to show you how and give you the tools to do it.

It's not just a matter of WHAT your profit margin is but WHEN you make it. If your margin is too thin or locked up in retainage, you're impairing your team's ability to perform at their peak and limiting your company's ability to grow, or worse you may even be putting your company in jeopardy by limiting the free cash flow to the overall business needs. Profit on paper is useless to you. It is even more worthless if you are never actually able to realize that profit into your bank account

What would the project's cash flow need to look like to increase efficiency in the project? What would it take for you to start the job with materials on site and a whatever size crew you wanted? What would two weeks of saved labor costs do for your bottom-line profit?

It can make a REAL difference.

CHAPTER 8:

COMMON FINANCE OPTIONS EXPLAINED

ONE OF THE MOST COMMON mistakes business owners make is to view debt as a thing to fear rather than as a tool for growth. The reality is plenty of business owners borrow money not because they need it to survive, but because it is the smartest way to capitalize on an opportunity, run the business, or manage the cash required to operate the business in the most effective way.

However, financial solutions are not one-size-fits-all. In order to build a financial plan that will allow you to run the business and support your plans for growth, it is important to use the right funding option for each opportunity. Using debt or other financial instruments for those purposes is excellent, however oftentimes business owners find themselves taking on debt to fix a problem or series of mistakes that were made instead. In these situations, debt can also be good and certainly can make the business owner and business feel a lot better, but it still may not be what the business needs to grow. Here is a list of funding sources your company can take advantage of, when it is best to use them, and when it is not.

THE TRADITIONAL BANK LINE OF CREDIT (LOC)

This is the gold standard in lending. If you have a bank line of credit, your company has solid financials and a proven track record of performance. You can use the money for anything, including financing the upfront expenses on a new job. Lines of Credit are meant to give you access to cash when you need it and then be paid back down when you are paid from the work you do. A bank wants to see the LOC drawn on and paid back down frequently. They do not want to see it used like a long-term loan. That means using it to bridge the gap in times cash is needed is ideal. Making payroll every week before you are able to invoice a project, paying the supplier bill that is due this week but you will not receive your payment for that material till next month, or investing the cash needed into some pre-construction work for a new project you will not be able to invoice for 30-60 days. These are ideal uses for a LOC as opposed to buying a new piece of equipment that you need. However, if you have a great opportunity to buy a piece of equipment you need and it required you to pay cash for it in order to take advantage of that opportunity then the LOC would be an excellent tool for that purpose, however you must be disciplined to do two things, (1) immediately start the process to get an equipment loan and (2) when you do get the equipment loan you use that money to pay the LOC back down. The downside to a LOC is this: The size of your Line of Credit is typically determined by your past 24 months financial performance, not the next 24 months.

If you are growing fast, you may outgrow your line of credit and need other forms of credit to help with the growth.

SBA LOAN - LONG TERM LOAN FROM A BANK WITH AN SBA GUARANTEE

First thing to know is the SBA does not issue loans, banks do. An "SBA loan" is the typical term that is used, but it is important to know this is really a loan from a bank that has approved your business and then received a guarantee from the SBA. What does a guarantee mean? Basically, it means that if the loan is made to you under certain terms and conditions that the SBA approves in advance, they will guarantee some portion of the loan the bank made to you. In the event you don't repay the loan the bank can go to the SBA to be repaid a portion of the loan (typically 80%).

These are often easier to acquire than a bank line of credit, IF you qualify as a small business. For commercial construction, the SBA defines a small business as one with no more than $39.5 million in average receipts. The loans also have maximum loan amounts and terms for repayment that need to be considered. SBA loans also require a LOT of documentation, and you need to find the right sponsor (i.e bank) to make it happen. The biggest downside in terms of growth is that once you hit the cap, you no longer qualify.

An important side note: Not all SBA loans, or banks that provide them, are the same! Finding the right bank to sponsor your SBA loan is very important and how they present your business is critical as well as how you present to them. The bank is still taking a risk on your SBA loan and their assessment of your business and the perceived credit risk is just as critical to the approval process. Build a relationship with your bank and your banker early in the life of your business. It is best to have these relationships in place long before you need a loan. If you do not have a relationship with a bank now and need to get a loan, you can find a good consultant that can help you who does have relationships with banks.

INVOICE FACTORING

Simply put, invoice factoring is a way to use the Accounts Receivables (the money you invoice your customers and they owe you for the work you performed) of the business to generate cash by selling those invoices to a factoring company. The factor will give you an advance on the amount that is owed to you (usually about 80%) and then they will wait to be paid by your customer under the normal terms of payment. When they receive payment from your customer they will take the fees that are owed to them and then remit the balance to you. This process can be repeated over and over each time you generate an invoice to your customer(s).

While invoice factoring shrinks the time between when you invoice and when you receive some cash, it doesn't get you funding before the work starts. And while financing your company between payments is absolutely a normal part of the construction industry, many subcontractors and general contractors have a negative perception of factoring. There are several reasons why general contractors have a negative view, but the most common reason is it affects the contractual terms they have with you in the subcontract agreement and their ability to set-off payments that are owed to you. When a factor purchases a receivable from you, they typically will require that the invoice is verified. The process of verifying that invoice involves the GC certifying they do in fact owe you the money invoiced and that they will pay that invoice when due and in full. It's that step of verification that the GC typically does not like as it removes their ability to set-off that payment in the future should they want to, based on something related to your performance on the job, a negative change order, or one of your vendors is required to be paid.

Invoice factoring CAN help you grow. Done right, it can balance out your unpredictable cash flow, which gives you a chance to fund more strategic growth initiatives.

ASSET-BASED LINES OF CREDIT

Like invoice factoring, an ABL line of credit can regulate cash flow by speeding up the time between invoice and payment. This allows you to have more cash in hand to run your project and overall business.

For both invoice factoring and ABL credit, you need to make sure you aren't paying for future growth with money you need for present demands. This is one reason we recommend setting up a dedicated payroll checking account, keeping your Operations account for just operations of the business. Invoice factoring and ABL lines of credit require great administrative capabilities in your business and financial discipline. When you receive money from your invoices it is critical to make sure you use the funds for the project you were advanced on—paying the subs, vendors, suppliers when you are paid. Maybe you don't pay them in full or you provide partial payments, but nonetheless the money you receive is marked for specific job-related costs and if you use the money for something else you will not have that money 30-45 days later when it is time to pay them and that can be the cause of major issues for you on that project. Then those major issues can carry over into the main business!

ABL lines of credit and factoring are great financing tools, but like any finance option, they must be used correctly and as designed or they can create problems in the business that are much worse for you. For example, these problems can occur if you do not manage your accounts payable properly when you receive money from the ABL line.

MERCHANT CASH ADVANCES

These have nearly ZERO benefit to construction contractor's plans for growth. In fact, these high-risk cash advances can destroy your ability to get paid for the job you're on now and crush any dreams of future growth. These are the daily or weekly payment "loans" that have been out and available for the past 10+ years. You can get funded very fast, in just a matter of 24-48 hours, and the deposit will come straight into your business operating account.

Here's how they work:

The MCA lender will assess the number of deposits and activity you have in your checking account on a monthly basis and then provide you an "advance" on those future deposits. They then add their advance fee to the amount that is being advanced to you (for construction that fee is typically between 33% - 50%). The repayment of the advance is typically between 6-12 months.

I am here to tell you as clearly as I possibly can this is NOT a financial product for construction contractors.

Don't believe me? Here's a quick story: A commercial glazier in Texas had a healthy balance sheet and a line of credit at his local bank. The line of credit had been in place for years, and was a little too small now for the size his business had become, but they were making due and all signs pointed to continued success.

Until there was a delay on a project, which resulted in a cash shortage. The owner needed to make payroll, so he found a quick and "easy" solution—a Merchant Cash Advance. And when he couldn't keep up with the daily payments, he got another advance. The daily payments coming out of his account doubled and the money from the deposit of the advance was the actual money being used to make the payments to the advance.

The easy and fast way to get money is not the best way for your company to finance itself. This Texas business owner almost went bankrupt. He almost lost everything. He did lose a lot, and that isn't even counting all the stress.

Bottom Line: Merchant cash advances don't work for construction companies.

MOBILIZATION FUNDING

Our loan program is designed to help a company execute the work they have available to them by providing access to cash at the start of a project or contract. When the company has revenue in the form of a contract, purchase orders, or a service agreement, we can help them. Our loans provide the money needed to pay for labor, materials or other project related costs before the company invoices their customer. This allows the company to get started on the project in the most efficient manner by removing the barrier of, "Do I have enough cash to do it the way it should be done?" They can get on a project with the right amount of labor, order the materials needed in the best form and timing, use the right equipment, and so on.

That means You, the owner, can do the work in the most efficient manner and not lose sleep about how you are going to make payroll each week or pay the vendors, subs, and suppliers.

Our construction financing program is built to help you grow. You can confidently bid on bigger projects because you know you won't have to finance the labor out of your own pocket. You can take on the extra work without putting a financial strain on the business, but still do the work and grow the business. Our loan structure is designed to be paid back as you get paid on the project.

Having a financial partner can greatly improve the strength of your company. A financial capability letter from that partner will also improve your bid, winning you more work.

We work with our clients to align our repayment plan to their pay apps, minimizing the strain of repaying a loan on top of managing your business. Finally, we have a network of experts in industries like insurance, legal, equipment, and more who are ready to help when one of our clients has a question.

CONCLUSION

I HOPE YOU HAVE FOUND the information in these pages helpful. One of our core values here at Mobilization Funding is, "Do the right thing," and after nearly 10 years financing commercial construction subcontractors, manufacturers, fabricators, and other businesses, we've learned a lot about the cash flow realities business owners face. Sharing it with everyone—through our blogs, guides, webinars, and now this book—certainly feels like the right thing to do.

I talk to business owners every day who are facing big challenges and big opportunities. I want to help as many people as I can overcome cash flow challenges, avoid bad cash flow decisions, and execute on those big opportunities.

Small and medium-sized businesses are the heart and soul of our country. Owning your own business is part of the American dream for so many people, but it can quickly become a nightmare when cash flow drags you down. I've seen business trouble ruin lives and destroy families. I don't want that to happen to anyone else. This book is my way of helping that to become a reality.

I also wanted to write this book so you know you are not alone. I can't tell you how often I talk to business owners who are hesitant to share that they took out an MCA, or scared to reveal how much debt they have, or feel ashamed of their inability to get ahead.

You're not alone. Running a business is tough, and chances are you got into the business because you love your trade or craft, not because you love accounting spreadsheets and cash flow models.

When you own your business, it can feel like you're doing it all on your own. You're not. Or, at least, you shouldn't. Everyone needs a little help. I have an amazing team, an accountant, a lawyer, mentors I trust, and a community of peers I can turn to. I can tell you honestly that it makes all the difference when times get tough.

Build your community. Find your mentors. Hire the experts you need so you can be the leader your team needs you to be.

Side note — If you're in construction and you're not on LinkedIn yet, I strongly encourage you to come check it out. There is a huge supportive community of construction professionals there, including me. I'm happy to be your first connection.

Do Your Part

Our country was built through construction. Every hospital, home, church, grocery store, road and school was built by the men and women of the construction industry. The Golden Gate Bridge, the Hoover Dam, and the White House—some of the most iconic places our country has to offer are here thanks to construction.

It used to be a source of pride to be part of the industry building America.

And it still IS. We've let other voices, outside voices, change the narrative. Construction has become the boogieman for high school guidance counselors and college admissions officers. *If you don't go to college, you'll end up digging ditches.*

Ridiculous. For starters, the dirt world is an incredible field and starting with an apprenticeship outside of high school is a great way to build a lasting career that puts food on your family's table and helps keep our country moving, literally. Check out my friends at BuildWitt (www.buildwitt.com) to see just how amazing.

More troubling is that this narrative around construction has affected the way we inside the industry think about ourselves.

We stopped trusting each other. We stopped believing what we once knew to be true — that the industry is filled with hardworking men and women who are defined by their integrity and their dedication to performance.

This new mindset became apparent to me over the years as I listened to hundreds if not thousands of subcontractors and general contractors talk about each other and others in the industry.

You can't trust the GC. They look for excuses not to pay us.

You can't trust subcontractors. Half of them never even finish the work.

And one day, I'd decided I'd had enough.

DO YOUR PART is about cleaning the slate. It's a return to the truth of construction. Because the truth is I work with subs and GCs every day, and on both sides there are more good apples than bad.

You can learn more about Do Your Part and join us by signing the pledge on our website: www.mobilizationfunding.com/do-your-part

The Power of Giving

YOU ARE HAPPIEST WHEN YOU are giving when you are helping someone else. Gratitude is such a dopamine kick. You are happy when you make others happy. I believe that. I KNOW that.

The whole world is connected. When you help someone, it doesn't mean that person will come back and help you. They might, but that's not the point. What does happen is that your help impacts that person, who impacts someone else, and the ripples expand further and further out. And eventually the help comes back to you.

It's part of why I wrote this book. It makes me feel GREAT knowing I am sharing tools and information and helping people achieve their goals.

If you enjoyed this book and found the information useful, you can help me help more business owners by sharing a review on Amazon. Reviews tell Amazon the book is worthwhile, so it shows up in more searches.

Thank you for reading. I appreciate you.

ABOUT MOBILIZATION FUNDING

Who We Are

Since 2013, we have been the lender who says Yes when the banks say No. Our reputation is built upon the merit of our loan program and the strength of our team.

While we all have different backgrounds and perspectives, we are united by our core values and driven by our purpose.

What We Do

We specialize in contract and purchase order financing for commercial construction subcontractors, manufacturers, and fabricators.

We provide the working capital you need when you need it MOST — at the beginning of a project. We work with you to build a repayment schedule, so you pay us when you get paid. Makes sense, right?

Why We Do It

"To help people in order to make their lives better" is our company's purpose and our passion. Whether that help comes through one of our loans, a referral to a trusted partner, or just some strategic advice, we are in the business of helping commercial construction contractors, and the entire construction industry, achieve their full potential!

MOBILIZATION FUNDING CORE VALUES

Create The Best Customer Experience

Leadership Through Action

Do The Right Thing

Be Humble

Commitment to Excellence

ABOUT THE AUTHOR

SCOTT CO-FOUNDED MOBILIZATION FUNDING IN 2013. It was Scott's vision and strategy that transitioned a series of investments into the successful business Mobilization Funding is today. He, alongside his team, oversees every aspect of the company to make sure they have a positive impact on everyone they meet.

Prior to Mobilization Funding, Scott spent 17 years in the medical device industry, where he held numerous positions in Sales, Sales Management, Corporate Contracting, and Executive Management. Before entering the medical device industry, he was the founder and principal of a small health and fitness company called the Wellness Zone that focused primarily on individual wellness programs for executives. Scott received his Bachelor's degree in Business with a concentration in Marketing and Hospitality Management from Keuka College in New York, although he credits his education to the books he has read and what he has learned from his mentors, most specifically the Arete Syndicate, led by Andy Frisella and Ed Mylett.

RESOURCES

You can find everything referenced in this book on this one page: www.mobilizationfunding.com/cashflow-book-resources

Mobilization Funding: www.mobilizationfunding.com

Do Your Part Pledge: www.mobilizationfunding.com/do-your-part

Cash Flow URL: www.mobilizationfunding.com/cashflow

Podcast: The Construction MF'ers Podcast, available everywhere you get your podcasts

MF YouTube Channel: www.youtube.com/mobilizationfunding